FIRED UP...FIRED UP

FIRED

UP!

A Collection of Campaign Prose
for President Obama That
Highlights His Great Works
That's Seldom Mentioned
Through The Media

VERONICA ELIZABETH SPIGNER

Published and Distributed by:
Professional Publishing House
1425 W. Manchester Blvd., Suite B
Los Angeles, California 90047
www.professionalpublishinghouse.com
Drrosie@aol.com
(323) 750-3592

Cover design :
First printing : September 2012
ISBN: 978-0-9853259-9-2
10987654321

Dedications

This book is dedicated to all who believe in liberty and justice for all Americans in every aspect, and to those who believe in the "Pledge of Allegiance" to the flag of America

May this book help bring back the enthusiasm and the excitement of the Obama voters in 2008. And may the 2012 first time Obama voters along with the returning '08 Obama voters for 2012, repeat or surpass the history-making voter's turnout by the Obama voters of 2008.

Thank Yous

I want to thank Dr. Rosie, owner of Professional Publishing House, for publishing my very first book.

And I want to thank Mama Green and my family and friends whom after reading my first handwritten book draft, gave me positive feedback and encouraging words.

In Memoriam

In Loving Memory of my deceased father, Truitt Sr. and my deceased mother, Audrey. Also, In Loving Memory of my dear friend, Joyce Simmons, who passed this year.

NOTES FROM THE AUTHOR

This *Fired Up!* book was first written as a song completed on July 20, 1994. I am inspired by Edith Childs, the "Chant Lady from Greenwood, S.C. with her "Fired Up, ready to go!" chant, to rewrite the lyrics to my "Fired Up!" melody I wrote 18 years ago, into a book for the Obama 2012 Presidential Campaign.

Because President Obama list of accomplishments are so long, this book condenses his achievements into several poetic verses. If anyone wants to know what our President has done, this song/book highlights his work in an informative, an educational, an exciting and fun manner.

Let's continue to Fire Up! The Democratic base and let's make voter's turnout history again on November 6, 2012 and beyond.

Below are my references:
1). Bill Press - "The Obama Hate Machine"
2). On the Internet - list of "Obama's 50 Great Accomplishments"
3). On the Internet - list of "244 Accomplishments of Pres. Obama" (1st printing)

CHANGES IN THE VOTING PROCEDURES CAN COME IN A VARIETY OF WAYS SUCH AS:

Illegal manipulations of voting machines
Photo Voter I.D. laws
Voting machine malfunctions
Voting locations opening late
Voting locations closing early
Not enough ballots
Disinformation of voting procedures
No paper ballots available

Encourage Provisional Ballots
No early voting
Purging voting rolls
Dishonest robo phone calls
Prevent voter registration efforts
Say police to make arrest at polls
Discarding registration forms
Felon disenfranchisement
Caging list
Phone jamming scandals
...and more

MAIN CHORUS

FIRED UP!
OBAMA'S ON FIRE!
FIRED UP!
OBAMA'S ON FIRE!
FIRED UP!
HE'S FIRED UP!
FIRED UP!
HE'S FIRED UP!

FIRED UP!
ObamaCares
FIRED UP!
For You and Me!
Don't you see Tea Party don't care
They rather see us fail, and be broke and bleed

(Chorus and Verses)

(1)PRESIDENT

Let me tell you something that takes great precedence
In '08 America voted for our First Black President
Right Wing Tea Party don't like it, but they're crazy and
ain't got no sense
Day one proposed Guantanamo Bay
Most impressive first 100 days
He **PASSED** the Historical Health Care Bill
Closed the donut hole on prescription pills
No pre-existing conditions when you get ill

FIRED UP!
OBAMA'S ON FIRE!
FIRED UP!
OBAMA'S ON FIRE!
FIRED UP!
HE'S FIRED UP!
FIRED UP!
HE'S FIRED UP!

**CASE CLOSED! NOW LEAVE MY
PRESIDENT ALONE!!!**

**FIRED UP!
5 Judges
FIRED UP!
Supreme Court
FIRED UP!
Upheld the Decision
Tea Party the ones that came up short**

(2)PRESIDENT

At the Boston Democratic Convention there was a speaker
that was unknown
In that year 2004 when he spoke he became the star of the show
At the Old State Capitol like Lincoln he announced his Presidency
On Inauguration Day
1.8 million People stayed
To **CELEBRATE** the First Black President
Who will win Re-Election—a second Term
Like FDR and Clinton did when it was their turn

FIRED UP!
OBAMA'S ON FIRE!
FIRED UP!
OBAMA'S ON FIRE!
FIRED UP!
HE'S FIRED UP!
FIRED UP!
HE'S FIRED UP!

FIRED UP!
Control the House and Senate
FIRED UP!
This time around
FIRED UP!
Cause Obama's Re-Election in 2012
Is standing on solid ground

(3)PRESIDENT

Mr. Obama got married to a beautiful Black Queen Michelle
Their girls—Malia and Sasha—are adorable as well
They live as a family in The White House in D.C.
Kiss cam got them on the second round
Where Black on Black Love can be found
He **SANG** "Let's Stay Together" so smooth
With a rhythmic grove and a soulful sound
He's wearing those shades being Black cool

FIRED UP!
OBAMA'S ON FIRE!
FIRED UP!
OBAMA'S ON FIRE!
FIRED UP!
HE'S FIRED UP!
FIRED UP!
HE'S FIRED UP!

FIRED UP!
The President stopped smoking
FIRED UP!
An example for you
FIRED UP!
In the White House garden
First Lady Obama says, Let's Move!

(4)BUDGETING

President Clinton left a 236-million-dollars surplus
Clinton did it by taxing the rich like radio fat man name Rush
"W." turned the Surplus into a trillion dollars deficit
In 2000 Bush didn't even win
In '04 back at cheat'n again
Obama is **CLEANING** up Bush's mess
So don't blame Obama he's passed the test
With this Republican-Controlled Congress he's doing his best

FIRED UP!
OBAMA'S ON FIRE!
FIRED UP!
OBAMA'S ON FIRE!
FIRED UP!
HE'S FIRED UP!
FIRED UP!
HE'S FIRED UP!

FIRED UP!
A brand new focus
FIRED UP!
On mortgage fraud
FIRED UP!
No more tax benefits to
Companies that outsource jobs

(5)REPUBLICONS

The last part of Republican(t) is spelled c-a-n
Gonna change the "A" to an "O" to pronounce their name Republi**cons**
They lie and cheat and hate to be beat and illegally steal <u>money</u>
The Republicons are a Party of NO
Tea Party's the same and they're hateful and cold
The Republicons **BLOCKED** 497 Bills
Tea Party don't care about the facts
And how the American people feel

FIRED UP!
OBAMA'S ON FIRE!
FIRED UP!
OBAMA'S ON FIRE!
FIRED UP!
HE'S FIRED UP!
FIRED UP!
HE'S FIRED UP!

FIRED UP!
Tea Party don't want
To raise taxes
All they want to do is sit down
On their Hands and Asses *(Assets)*

(6)BOEHNER (Boner)

The Grand Old Party Republicon men are much less to be desired
They have Boehner (Boner) Speaker of the House who's just a
great big crier
They all play Dirty Politics, their names on a laundry list
Bush, Cheney, Romney, Ryan and Rove
Hannity, Canter, Mitchell, O'Reilly and more
The Republicons don't **WANT** Bush Jr. Tax breaks to stop
If anyone can afford to pay their taxes
It's the wealthiest and richest 1% at the top

FIRED UP!
OBAMA'S ON FIRE!
FIRED UP!
OBAMA'S ON FIRE!
FIRED UP!
HE'S FIRED UP!
FIRED UP!
HE'S FIRED UP!

Obstruction

FIRED UP!
Right Wing Congress
Don't want to get anything done
They have a Speaker of the House
Who even cried when he won

(7)BIRTHERS

Whomever birth the Birthers' name the movement should have
Never been born
Funded by the Koch brothers and others
Donald Trumpet had the loudest horn
Koch brothers have family foundations, Cato,
Heritage Institute and more
Tea Party has erroneous views
Fox and Friends is where they get their views
They **REFUSE** to pass the Jobs Bill and reduce the deficit
That will help the poor and the Middle Class
Get their financial budget and personal needs met

FIRED UP!
OBAMA'S ON FIRE!
FIRED UP!
OBAMA'S ON FIRE!
FIRED UP!
HE'S FIRED UP!
FIRED UP!
HE'S FIRED UP!

FIRED UP!
On NOV. the 6th
FIRED UP!
Take back the House
FIRED UP!
Creating jobs for the Poor and Middle Class
Is what Obama is all about

(8)BIRTHERS

The Birthers' getting a brand new name but on
Fox News the talk is mute
Congressman Yoder in the Sea of Galilee took a
dip in his Birthers' suit
President Obama a born again Christian was
Born in the USA
Being a Christian mean you should show your Love
Phileo style that comes from God above
The Republicons are the **BIGGEST** HYPOCRITES
Like the Pharisee in ancient days
And their presidential candidate name Mitt

FIRED UP!
OBAMA'S ON FIRE!
FIRED UP!
OBAMA'S ON FIRE!
FIRED UP!
HE'S FIRED UP!
FIRED UP!
HE'S FIRED UP!

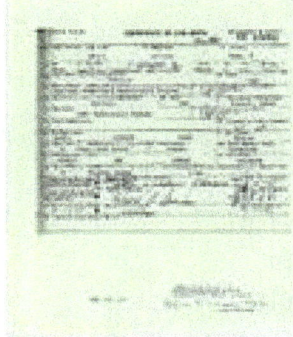

FIRED UP!
Grade is Incomplete
FIRED UP!
Need 4 More Years
FIRED UP!
To complete the job in creating more jobs
To calm all your tears and fears

(9)THE HATERS

It just so happen when Obama ran and
won The President
It exposed the bigoted racist that came
out of the closet
With the Secret Service the kind of protection Obama
needs come from God you cannot see
Tea baggers want Obama's fate
But God protects him from the harm and the hate
If it's **GOD'S** Will for a Second Term
The GOP Senate and House seats will squirm
The Koch brothers Republicons will never learn

FIRED UP!
OBAMA'S ON FIRE!
FIRED UP!
OBAMA'S ON FIRE!
FIRED UP!
HE'S FIRED UP!
FIRED UP!
HE'S FIRED UP!

FIRED UP!
God Is
FIRED UP!
In Control
The Right Wing think they know
it all but God is the ONE that Runs the Show

(10)REPUBLICON GOVERNORS

The Republicon Governors re-election in the year 2012
No different than the Romney/Ryan ticket they hit below
the political belt
Romney running those lying ads cause he knows he's one himself
Obama/Biden ads tells the truth
Can't dispute the facts the views are true
Romney nose is **GROWING** like Pinocchio
Vote out the GOP Governors
From the north to the south and from coast to coast

FIRED UP!
OBAMA'S ON FIRE!
FIRED UP!
OBAMA'S ON FIRE!
FIRED UP!
HE'S FIRED UP!
FIRED UP!
HE'S FIRED UP!

FIRED UP!
Gov. Jan Brewer
Step back and give him space
And take your boney little finger
Out of my President's face

(11)ECONOMY

Obama signed the American Recovery and Reinvestment Act
Created Jobs and gave tax cuts for the Working and the Middle Class
He doubled the child tax credit in the year 2010
Going Forward not Backwards with trust
Passed the Wall Street Reform for us
The President **SAVED** the Auto Industry
GM and Chrysler gain in the Market profits
The Cash for Clunkers Program was also a BIG hit

FIRED UP!
OBAMA'S ON FIRE!
FIRED UP!
OBAMA'S ON FIRE!
FIRED UP!
HE'S FIRED UP!
FIRED UP!
HE'S FIRED UP!

FIRED UP!
Hilda Solis
FIRED UP!
Labor Secretary
FIRED UP!
Public sector jobs, nurses,
Teachers, fire and the police

(12)ECONOMY

Obama ended Bush policies that protected Credit Cards and
Wall Street companies
Now we have protection for Consumers that stop "Banksters"
from raising their fees
Since Reagan fairy trickle down dust hasn't
trickled down to us yet
Obama signed the Hire Act
For Small Businesses he reduced their tax
When they **HIRE** the unemployed
Economic recovery will grow overtime
The Unemployment Numbers will begin to decline

FIRED UP!
OBAMA'S ON FIRE!
FIRED UP!
OBAMA'S ON FIRE!
FIRED UP!
HE'S FIRED UP!
FIRED UP!
HE'S FIRED UP!

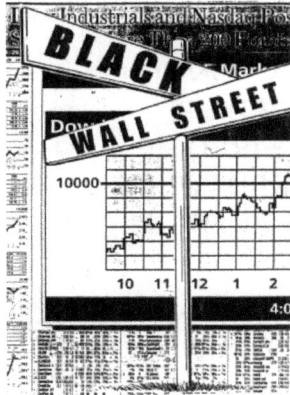

FIRED UP!
Manufacturing jobs
FIRED UP!
Made in the USA
FIRED UP!
Ford, Jazz, and apple pie
Is the old-fashioned American way

(13)EDUCATION

Investment Federal funding for Science and Research Labs
The highest amount student borrower must pay the President
placed a cap
Increased funding available for Student Loans in 2009
Streamlined the Federal Student Loan process
Cut out the middle banks so students pay less
The President **LAUNCHED** "Educate to Innovate"
For Science, Mathematics, and Technology
Broadband Internet with the high speed

FIRED UP!
OBAMA'S ON FIRE!
FIRED UP!
OBAMA'S ON FIRE!
FIRED UP!
HE'S FIRED UP!
FIRED UP!
HE'S FIRED UP!

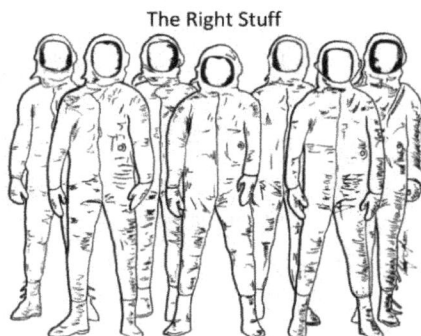

The Right Stuff

FIRED UP!
Race to the Top
FIRED UP!
That sets the high bar
FIRED UP!
A belated birthday present from
NASA and Curiosity landed on Mars

(14)EPA (Disaster Relief)

Prior to Katrina Bush Jr. removed FEMA from directly
reporting to him
This fact sounds suspicious to me and boy
I smell a rat
Bush family don't like Black people Kanye
I second that
President Obama restored FEMA again
To help the children, families, women and men
He ordered a **REVIEW** of Disaster Preparedness
Not like George W. who left a mess
Give medical, food, and shelter so the Survivors can be blessed

FIRED UP!
OBAMA'S ON FIRE!
FIRED UP!
OBAMA'S ON FIRE!
FIRED UP!
HE'S FIRED UP!
FIRED UP!
HE'S FIRED UP!

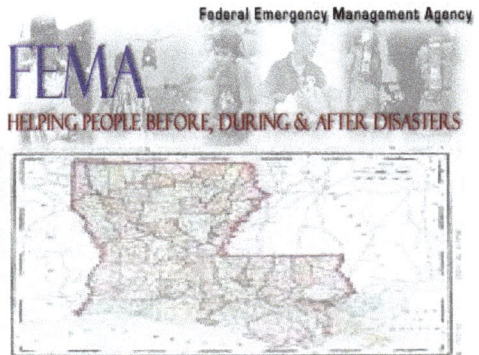

Federal Emergency Management Agency

FEMA

HELPING PEOPLE BEFORE, DURING & AFTER DISASTERS

FIRED UP!
The President invest
FIRED UP!
In Renewable Energy
FIRED UP!
Federal Green Agencies to decrease
The effects of Global Warming

(15)FOREIGN POLICY

Ended 30 year Mubarak reign and 42 year rule of Muammar Gaddafi
He signed with Russia and won ratification to achieve the
New Start Treaty
President Obama helped improve America's Image in
10 out of 15 countries
Bush Jr. said "dead or alive"
But it was Obama who got the prize
The Commander in Chief **KILLED**
Osama Bin Laden
Ordered the Navy Seals Special Forces
"W" as president will be forgotten

FIRED UP!
OBAMA'S ON FIRE!
FIRED UP!
OBAMA'S ON FIRE!
FIRED UP!
HE'S FIRED UP!
FIRED UP!
HE'S FIRED UP!

FIRED UP!
Awarded the
FIRED UP!
Nobel Peace Prize
FIRED UP!
Gave the Prize Money
To several of his favorite Charities

(16)MILITARY and VETERANS

President Obama increased support for our Veterans
New G.I. Bill for returning Veterans from
Iraq and Afghanistan
Ordered that conditions of Walter Reed Hospital and other
facilities be improved
Drawdown of war in Afghanistan
Trying to stop nuclear war with Iran
He kept his **PROMISE** to get out of Iraq
Ordered better Body Armor to protect our troops
With new Mime Resistant Vehicles
against an ambush

FIRED UP!
OBAMA'S ON FIRE!
FIRED UP!
OBAMA'S ON FIRE!
FIRED UP!
HE'S FIRED UP!
FIRED UP!
HE'S FIRED UP!

REMEMBER OUR VETERANS

FIRED UP!
Established a New
FIRED UP!
Task Force to assist
FIRED UP!
For Federal contracts and improve access
To all our Veterans who own a Business

(17)MITT ROMNEY

Romney has riches and wealth the 1% and he has the Super PACs
He does more flip-flopping than pancakes
and a waffle stack
Tea Party are a bunch of party poopers the London Games were
filled with Romney Bloopers
Romney saved his Olympics with Gov't money
Didn't build it by himself he needed help you see
Romney got less than an **OUNCE** from his Convention Bounce
Mittens say we built it
Leaving out the history Black slaves helped it

FIRED UP!
OBAMA'S ON FIRE!
FIRED UP!
OBAMA'S ON FIRE!
FIRED UP!
HE'S FIRED UP!
FIRED UP!
HE'S FIRED UP!

The Star
IS FALLEN
is fallen

FIRED UP!
Obama Ordered
FIRED UP!
The closing of
FIRED UP!
Tax safe havens
For business tax evaders

(18)MIT ROMNEY

They want to repeal ObamaCare with Medicare Vouchers and
privatize Social Security
That's why Mitt Romney chose Paul Ryan as his choice for V.P.
Paul Ryan is a jerk McCain and Palin didn't work a mistake
says Dick Cheney
Bain closed U.S. Companies
To gain more profits in jobs Overseas
Romney is the **OUTSOURCE** in Chief
Says a British newspaper in London
There's nothing "Romney Hood" wouldn't do
under the sun

FIRED UP!
OBAMA'S ON FIRE!
FIRED UP!
OBAMA'S ON FIRE!
FIRED UP!
HE'S FIRED UP!
FIRED UP!
HE'S FIRED UP!

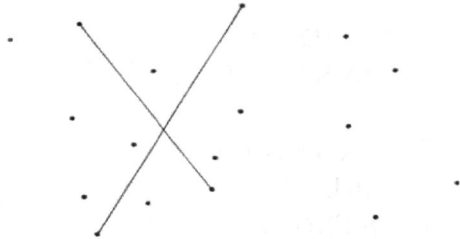

Connect the Dots

FIRED UP!
We ought to stop
FIRED UP!
Overseas call centers
FIRED UP!
To Create More Insource jobs
For the American people to have and enter

(19)PAUL RYAN

The GOP have Pain in the Aiken a position they have Taken but
they're trying to run away from it
Too late sorry V.P. Paul Ryan ALL of Aiken's views to you will stick
It's a crying shame and a new political low that Sarah Palin is a
better pick
Selecting Ryan didn't get the bounce
The political scale moved just an ounce
The Republicons have waged a **WAR** on Women
The rolling back of our rights must end
See Emily's list to know who're their friends

FIRED UP!
OBAMA'S ON FIRE!
FIRED UP!
OBAMA'S ON FIRE!
FIRED UP!
HE'S FIRED UP!
FIRED UP!
HE'S FIRED UP!

FIRED UP!
Don't be fooled
By Paul Ryan's charm
His beliefs and policies are so extreme
Written and made to do you harm

(20)REPUBLICON'S CONVENTION 2012 (Tampa, Fl)

The Republicon Convention was delayed for a day due to
Hurricane Isaac
No Bush or Cheney in the audience and where're the Black people at
On one hand their Herman Cain, Artur Davis,
Mia Love and Condoleezza Rice
Ann Romney says we built it
Leaving out the fact that Bain Outsource it
Go Ahead Obama and Make Your **DAY** in Charlotte, North Carolina
For the 2012 Democratic Convention
We Out Bounced Tampa before we were done

FIRED UP!
OBAMA'S ON FIRE!
FIRED UP!
OBAMA'S ON FIRE!
FIRED UP!
HE'S FIRED UP!
FIRED UP!
HE'S FIRED UP!

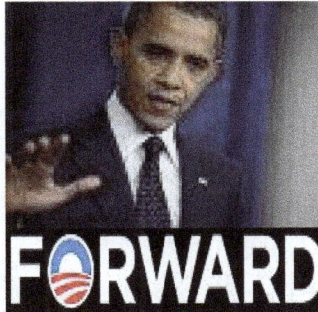

FIRED UP!
Didn't it seem
Rubio and Christie
Instead of Romney running for the presidency

(21)DEMOCRATIC WOMEN

Former Tea Party members are coming
to the Democratic side
Realized can't have their own minds must stick to talking
points and lies
Palin, Bachmann, O'Donnell, and Malkin are unqualified and
should also quit
Democratic women are strong and bold
Don't have to be led or what should be told
God **SAVED** Congresswoman Gabby's life
Waters, Pelosi, Boxer, and Lee
The best Secretary of State is a woman, Hillary

FIRED UP!
OBAMA'S ON FIRE!
FIRED UP!
OBAMA'S ON FIRE!
FIRED UP!
HE'S FIRED UP!
FIRED UP!
HE'S FIRED UP!

The Best Man for the Job, is a Woman

FIRED UP!
Obama knows
FIRED UP!
What a woman need
Don't be taken by Ryan looks
Cause he's no Kennedy

(22)MISCELLANEOUS

Our President used his executive orders to help
The Historical HBCUs
Our "Mind is a terrible thing to waste" these schools are
here to educate you
Obama signed the Ledbetter Equality Law so the women
can get Fair Pay
A former Senator from Illinois
Come on Hispanics and join us Hoy
The President **SIGNED** U.S. Manufacturing Enhancement Act
Appointed Sotomayor and Elena Kagen
To the Highest Supreme Court in all the land

FIRED UP!
OBAMA'S ON FIRE!
FIRED UP!
OBAMA'S ON FIRE!
FIRED UP!
HE'S FIRED UP!
FIRED UP!
HE'S FIRED UP!

"Conservative Compassion?"
"¿Compasión Conservador?"

FIRED UP!
5 Judges
FIRED UP!
Supreme Court
FIRED UP!
Upheld the Decision the Tea Party
The ones that came up short

(23)DEMOCRATIC CONVENTION 2012

First Lady Michelle Obama gave an amazing speech at this
year's DNC
Told how her husband lived the American Dream and his
vision to save the world
She has poise, grace and dignity without even wearing her pearls
YES WE CAN! Do it again!
Hope and Change we still believe in
We **CRIED** when Gabby gave the
Pledge of Allegiance
Go, Joe, Go in the Fired Up! Band
A much better V.P. than Joe Loserman

FIRED UP!
JOE BIDEN'S ON FIRE!
FIRED UP!
JOE BIDEN'S ON FIRE!
FIRED UP!
HE'S FIRED UP!
FIRED UP!
HE'S FIRED UP!

FIRED UP!
Bin Laden is dead
FIRED UP!
GM is alive
FIRED UP!
Going FORWARD not Back,
let's give a HIGH FIVE
With Obama's Administration
we will SURVIVE

(24)NORTH CAROLINA, DNC 2012

In Charlotte, North Carolina at school
we were taught
By former President Bill Clinton whose Legacy is Greater
than we thought
Mrs. Clinton Secretary of State and he's
"Secretary of Explaining Stuff"
President Obama also gave a great speech
Just enough and that did it for me
Obama got a **NINE** percent Bounce
From the 2012 Democratic Convention
Unlike the RNC that got no action

FIRED UP!
BILL CLINTON'S ON FIRE!
FIRED UP!
BILL CLINTON'S ON FIRE!
FIRED UP!
HE'S FIRED UP!
FIRED UP!
HE'S FIRED UP!

Monica Who?

YOUR

LEGACY

WILL

STILL

STAND

RESILIENT
CHARACTER

FIRED UP!
Obama Passed
FIRED UP!
The Arithmetic Test
FIRED UP!
Don't want Double Down on Triple Down
So Re-elect Obama for the 2nd Round

(25)VOTER SUPPRESSION

The Headlines say Romney "Never Paid
Less than 13%"
The kind of money he has, to him it is
pennys and cents
The opposition has plans in place for widespread VOTER SUPPRESSION
Women Suffrage kept it Alive
Courageous Black People Bled and Died
To give us the **RIGHT** to Vote
So go to the Polls to cast your Vote
And don't be left out being the goat

FIRED UP!
OBAMA'S ON FIRE!
FIRED UP!
OBAMA'S ON FIRE!
FIRED UP!
HE'S FIRED UP!
FIRED UP!
HE'S FIRED UP!

FIRED UP!
Calling First Time Voters
FIRED UP!
'08 Voters coming back
FIRED UP!
If you haven't voted in over 4 years
Get your Democratic ballots and get on track

(26)GET-OUT-THE-VOTE (GOTV)

Obama won the popular vote over 8.5 Million
And he won the Electoral College that gave him a legitimate win
We're working like elves in 2012 'cause the GOP will try to steal
Independent Voters Obama's our Man
He's doing the Best he Can
We must **GET**-Out-The-Vote!
Start the ball rolling where Acorn stopped
And show Fox News they're Not on Top

FIRED UP!
OBAMA'S ON FIRE!
FIRED UP!
OBAMA'S ON FIRE!
FIRED UP!
HE'S FIRED UP!
FIRED UP!
HE'S FIRED UP!

I'm (still) praying for you
Mr. President!

FIRED UP!
Don't STOP!
FIRED UP!
Keep on PUSHING!
FIRED UP!
We must mobilize to give
Obama that CHEATN' CUSHION

(27)GET-OUT-THE-VOTE (GOTV)

"Dreams of My Father" and "The Audacity of Hope" are 2 books that
The President wrote
To give America Life Skills and different ways
we can cope
Because he knows the Republicons don't care all they gave him was
Hell *(Heck)* & Nope
We need to Get-Out-The-Vote
To continue Change that gave us Hope
Let's take **BACK** The House
The 47 % are not victims
And we're gonna Vote these Rascals OUT!

FIRED UP!
OBAMA'S ON FIRE!
FIRED UP!
OBAMA'S ON FIRE!
FIRED UP!
HE'S FIRED UP!
FIRED UP!
HE'S FIRED UP!

VOTE **ALL**
the RASCALS
OUT !!!

FIRED UP!
We're Much Better Off
FIRED UP!
Than 4 Years Ago
And Romney better not STOP
The funds for Big Bird and Elmo

(28)GET-OUT-THE-VOTE (GOTV)

Super PACs with Citizens United out spends Democrats 6 to 1
The Republicons think they can buy an election and that their
work is done
The Dems must match these Super PACs with People Power and a
lot of Fun
Let's go and knock on doors
Do the phone banks and call some more
Let's have FUN with this song
Let's Dance, and Sing and Shout
There's no putting Obama's Fire Out!

FIRED UP!
OBAMA'S ON FIRE!
FIRED UP!
OBAMA'S ON FIRE!
FIRED UP!
HE'S FIRED UP!
FIRED UP!
HE'S FIRED UP!

REMATCH
ELECTION 2012

FIRED UP!
OBAMA'S ON FIRE!
FIRED UP!
OBAMA'S ON FIRE!
FIRED UP!
HE'S FIRED UP!
FIRED UP!
HE'S FIRED UP!
FIRED UP!
HE'S FIRED UP!
FIRED UP! And Ready to Go!FIRED UP!

(Verses Only)

(1)PRESIDENT

Let me tell you something that takes great precedence
In '08 America voted for our First Black President
Right Wing Tea Party don't like it, but they're crazy and
ain't got no sense
Day one proposed Guantanamo Bay
Most impressive first 100 days
He **PASSED** the Historical Health Care Bill
Closed the donut hole on prescription pills
No pre-existing conditions when you get ill

(2)PRESIDENT
At the Boston Democratic Convention there was a speaker
that was unknown
In that year 2004 when he spoke he became the star of the show
At the Old State Capitol like Lincoln he announced his Presidency
On Inauguration Day
1.8 million People stayed
To **CELEBRATE** the First Black President
Who will win Re-Election—a second Term
Like FDR and Clinton did when it was their turn

(3)PRESIDENT
Mr. Obama got married to a beautiful Black Queen Michelle
Their girls—Malia and Sasha—are adorable as well
They live as a family in The White House in D.C.
Kiss cam got them on the second round
Where Black on Black Love can be found
He **SANG** "Let's Stay Together" so smooth
With a rhythmic grove and a soulful sound
He's wearing those shades being Black cool

(4)BUDGETING

President Clinton left a 236-million-dollars surplus
Clinton did it by taxing the rich like radio fat man name Rush
"W". turned the Surplus into a trillion dollars deficit
In 2000 Bush didn't even win
In '04 back at cheat'n again
Obama is **CLEANING** up Bush's mess
So don't blame Obama he's passed the test
With this Republican-Controlled Congress he's doing his best

(5)REPUBLICONS

The last part of Republi<u>can</u>(t) is spelled c-a-n
Gonna change the "A" to an "O" to pronounce their name Republi**cons**
They lie and cheat and hate to be beat and illegally steal <u>money</u>
The Republicons are a Party of NO
Tea Party's the same and they're hateful and cold
The Republicons **BLOCKED** 497 Bills
Tea Party don't care about the facts
And how the American people feel

(6)BOEHNER (Boner)

The Grand Old Party Republicon men are much less to be desired
They have Boehner (Boner) Speaker of the House who's just a
great big crier
They all play Dirty Politics, their names on a laundry list
Bush, Cheney, Romney, Ryan and Rove
Hannity, Canter, Mitchell, O'Reilly and more
The Republicons don't **WANT** Bush Jr. Tax breaks to stop
If anyone can afford to pay their taxes
It's the wealthiest and richest 1% at the top

(7)BIRTHERS

Whomever birth the Birthers' name the movement should have
Never been born
Funded by the Koch brothers and others
Donald Trumpet had the loudest horn

Koch brothers have family foundations, Cato,
Heritage Institute and more
Tea Party has erroneous views
Fox and Friends is where they get their views
They **REFUSE** to pass the Jobs Bill and reduce the deficit
That will help the poor and the Middle Class
Get their financial budget and personal needs met

(8)BIRTHERS
The Birthers' getting a brand new name but on
Fox News the talk is mute
Congressman Yoder in the Sea of Galilee took a
dip in his Birthers' suit
President Obama a born again Christian was
Born in the USA
Being a Christian mean you should your Love
Phileo style that comes from God above
The Republicons are the **BIGGEST** HYPOCRITES
Like the Pharisee in ancient days
And their presidential candidate name Mitt

(9)THE HATERS
It just so happen when Obama ran and
won The President
It exposed the bigoted racist that came
out of the closet
With the Secret Service the kind of protection Obama
needs come from God you cannot see
Tea baggers want Obama's fate
But God protects him from the harm and the hate
If it's **GOD'S** Will for a Second Term
The GOP Senate and House seats will squirm
The Koch brothers Republicons will never learn

38

(10)REPUBLICON GOVENORS

The Republicon Governors re-election in the year 2012
No different than the Romney/Ryan ticket they hit below
the political belt
Romney running those lying ads cause he knows he's one himself
Obama/Biden ads tells the truth
Can't dispute the facts the views are true
Romney nose is **GROWING** like Pinocchio
Vote out the GOP Governors
From the north to the south and from coast to coast

(11)ECONOMY

Obama signed the American Recovery and Reinvestment Act
Created Jobs and gave tax cuts for the Working and the Middle Class
He doubled the child tax credit in the year 2010
Going Forward not Backwards with trust
Passed the Wall Street Reform for us
The President **SAVED** the Auto Industry
GM and Chrysler gain in the Market profits
The Cash for Clunkers Program was also a BIG hit

(12)ECONOMY

Obama ended Bush policies that protected Credit Cards and
Wall Street companies
Now we have protection for Consumers that stop "Banksters"
from raising their fees
Since Reagan fairy trickle down dust hasn't
trickled down to us yet
Obama signed the Hire Act
For Small Businesses he reduced their tax
When they **HIRE** the unemployed
Economic recovery will grow overtime
The Unemployment Numbers will begin to decline

(13)EDUCATION
Investment Federal funding for Science and Research Labs
The highest amount student borrower must pay the President
placed a cap
Increased funding available for Student Loans in 2009
Streamlined the Federal Student Loan process
Cut out the middle banks so students pay less
The President **LAUNCHED** "Educate to Innovate"
For Science, Mathematics, and Technology
Broadband Internet with the high speed

(14)EPA (Disaster Relief)
Prior to Katrina Bush Jr. removed FEMA from directly
reporting to him
This fact sounds suspicious to me and boy
I smell a rat
Bush family don't like Black people Kanye
I second that
President Obama restored FEMA again
To help the children, families, women and men
He ordered a **REVIEW** of Disaster Preparedness
Not like George W. who left a mess
Give medical, food, and shelter so the Survivors can be blessed

(15)FOREIGN POLICY
Ended 30 year Mubarak reign and 42 year rule of Muammar Gaddafi
He signed with Russia and won ratification to achieve the
New Start Treaty
President Obama helped improve America's Image in
10 out of 15 countries
Bush Jr. said "dead or alive"
But it was Obama who got the prize
The Commander in Chief **KILLED**
Osama Bin Laden
Ordered the Navy Seals Special Forces
"W" as president will be forgotten

40

(16)MILITARY and VETERANS
President Obama increased support for our Veterans
New G.I. Bill for returning Veterans from
Iraq and Afghanistan
Ordered that conditions of Walter Reed Hospital and other
facilities be improved
Drawdown of war in Afghanistan
Trying to stop nuclear war with Iran
He kept his **PROMISE** to get out of Iraq
Ordered better Body Armor to protect our troops
With new Mime Resistant Vehicles
against an ambush

(17)MITT ROMNEY
Romney has riches and wealth the 1% and he has the Super PACs
He does more flip-flopping than pancakes
and a waffle stack
Tea Party are a bunch of party poopers the London Games were
filled with Romney Bloopers
Romney saved his Olympics with Gov't money
Didn't build it by himself he needed help you see
Romney got less than an **OUNCE** from his Convention Bounce
Mittens say we built it
Leaving out the history Black slaves helped it

(18)MITT ROMNEY
They want to repeal ObamaCare with Medicare Vouchers and
privatize Social Security
That's why Mitt Romney chose Paul Ryan as his choice for V.P.
Paul Ryan is a jerk McCain and Palin didn't work a mistake
says Dick Cheney
Bain closed U.S. Companies
To gain more profits in jobs Overseas
Romney is the **OUTSOURCE** in Chief
Says a British newspaper in London

There's nothing "Romney Hood" wouldn't do
under the sun

(19)PAUL RYAN
The GOP have Pain in the Aiken a position they have Taken but
they're trying to run away from it
Too late sorry V.P. Paul Ryan ALL of Aiken's views to you will stick
It's a crying shame and a new political low that Sarah Palin is a
better pick
Selecting Ryan didn't get the bounce
The political scale moved just an ounce
The Republicons have waged a **WAR** on Women
The rolling back of our rights must end
See Emily's list to know who're their friends

(20)REPUBLICON'S CONVENTION 2012 (Tampa, Fl)
The Republicon Convention was delayed for a day due to
Hurricane Isaac
No Bush or Cheney in the audience and where're the Black people at
On one hand their Herman Cain, Artur Davis,
Mia Love and Condoleezza Rice
Ann Romney says we built it
Leaving out the fact that Bain Outsource it
Go Ahead Obama and Make Your **DAY** in Charlotte, North Carolina
For the 2012 Democratic Convention
We Out Bounced Tampa before we were done

(21)DEMOCRATIC WOMEN
Former Tea Party members are coming
to the Democratic side
Realized can't have their own minds must stick to talking
points and lies
Palin, Bachmann, O'Donnell, and Malkin are unqualified and
should also quit
Democratic women are strong and bold

Don't have to be led or what should be told
God **SAVED** Congresswoman Gabby's life
Waters, Pelosi, Boxer, and Lee
The best Secretary of State is a woman, Hillary

(22)MISCELLANEOUS
Our President used his executive orders to help
The Historical HBCUs
Our "Mind is a terrible thing to waste" these schools are
here to educate you
Obama signed the Ledbetter Equality Law so the women
can get Fair Pay
A former Senator from Illinois
Come on Hispanics and join us Hoy
The President **SIGNED** U.S. Manufacturing Enhancement Act
Appointed Sotomayor and Elena Kagen
To the Highest Supreme Court in all the land

(23)DEMOCRATIC CONVENTION 2012
First Lady Michelle Obama gave an amazing speech at this
year's DNC
Told how her husband lived the American Dream and his
vision to save the world
She has poise, grace and dignity without even wearing her pearls
YES WE CAN! Do it again!
Hope and Change we still believe in
We **CRIED** when Gabby gave the
Pledge of Allegiance
Go, Joe, Go in the Fired Up! Band
A much better V.P. than Joe Loserman

(24)NORTH CAROLINA, DNC 2012

In Charlotte, North Carolina at school
we were taught
By former President Bill Clinton whose Legacy is Greater
than we thought
Mrs. Clinton Secretary of State and he's
"Secretary of Explaining Stuff"
President Obama also gave a great speech
Just enough and that did it for me
Obama got a **NINE** percent Bounce
From the 2012 Democratic Convention
Unlike the RNC that got no action

(25)VOTER SUPPRESSION

The Headlines say Romney "Never Paid
Less than 13%"
The kind of money he has, to him it is
pennys and cents
The opposition has plans in place for widespread VOTER SUPPRESSION
Women Suffrage kept it Alive
Courageous Black People Bled and Died
To give us the **RIGHT** to Vote
So go to the Polls to cast your Vote
And don't be left out being the goat

(26)GET-OUT-THE-VOTE (GOTV)

Obama won the popular vote over 8.5 Million
And he won the Electoral College that gave him a legitimate win
We're working like elves in 2012 'cause the GOP will try to steal
Independent Voters Obama's our Man
He's doing the Best he Can
We must **GET**-Out-The-Vote!
Start the ball rolling where Acorn stopped
And show Fox News they're Not on Top

(27)GET-OUT-THE-VOTE (GOTV)

"Dreams of My Father" and "The Audacity of Hope" are 2 books that
The President wrote
To give America Life Skills and different ways
we can cope
Because he knows the Republicons don't care all they gave him was
Hell *(Heck)* & Nope
We need to Get-Out-The-Vote
To continue Change that gave us Hope
Let's take **BACK** The House
The 47% are not victims
And we're gonna Vote all of these Rascals OUT!

(28)GET-OUT-THE-VOTE (GOTV)

Super PACs with Citizens United out spends Democrats 6 to 1
The Republicons think they can buy an election and that their
work is done
The Dems must match these Super PACs with People Power
and a lot of Fun
Let's go and knock on doors
Do the phone banks and call some more
Let's have **FUN** with this song
Let's Dance, and Sing and Shout
There's no putting Obama's Fire Out!

(Chorus only)

MAIN CHORUS
FIRED UP!
OBAMA'S ON FIRE!
FIRED UP!
OBAMA'S ON FIRE!
FIRED UP!
HE'S FIRED UP!
FIRED UP!
HE'S FIRED UP!
FIRED UP!
ObamaCares
FIRED UP!
For You and Me!
Don't you see Tea Party don't care
They rather see us fail, and be broke and bleed

(1)PRESIDENT
FIRED UP!
OBAMA'S ON FIRE!
FIRED UP!
OBAMA'S ON FIRE!
FIRED UP!
HE'S FIRED UP!
FIRED UP!
HE'S FIRED UP!
FIRED UP!
5 Judges
FIRED UP!
Supreme Court
FIRED UP!
Upheld the Decision
Tea Party the ones that came up short

(2)PRESIDENT
FIRED UP!
OBAMA'S ON FIRE!
FIRED UP!
OBAMA'S ON FIRE!
FIRED UP!
HE'S FIRED UP!
FIRED UP!
HE'S FIRED UP!
FIRED UP!
Control the House and Senate
FIRED UP!
This time around
FIRED UP!
Cause Obama's Re-election in 2012
Is standing on solid ground

(3)PRESIDENT
FIRED UP!
OBAMA'S ON FIRE!
FIRED UP!
OBAMA'S ON FIRE!
FIRED UP!
HE'S FIRED UP!
FIRED UP!
HE'S FIRED UP!
FIRED UP!
The President stopped smoking
FIRED UP!
An example for you
FIRED UP!
In the White House garden
First Lady Obama says, Let's Move!

(4)BUDGETING
FIRED UP!
OBAMA'S ON FIRE!
FIRED UP!
OBAMA'S ON FIRE!
FIRED UP!
HE'S FIRED UP!
FIRED UP!
HE'S FIRED UP!
FIRED UP!
A brand new focus
FIRED UP!
On mortgage fraud
FIRED UP!
No more tax benefits to
Companies that outsource jobs

(5)REPUBLICONS
FIRED UP!
OBAMA'S ON FIRE!
FIRED UP!
OBAMA'S ON FIRE!
FIRED UP!
HE'S FIRED UP!
FIRED UP!
HE'S FIRED UP!
FIRED UP!
Tea Party don't want
To raise taxes
All they want to do is sit down
On their Hands and Asses *(Assets)*

(6)BOEHNER (Boner)
FIRED UP!
OBAMA'S ON FIRE!
FIRED UP!
OBAMA'S ON FIRE!
FIRED UP!
HE'S FIRED UP!
FIRED UP!
HE'S FIRED UP!
FIRED UP!
Right Wing Congress
Don't want to get anything done
They have a Speaker of the House
Who even cried when he won

(7)BIRTHERS
FIRED UP!
OBAMA'S ON FIRE!
FIRED UP!
OBAMA'S ON FIRE!
FIRED UP!
HE'S FIRED UP!
FIRED UP!
HE'S FIRED UP!
FIRED UP!
On NOV. the 6th
FIRED UP!
Take back the House
FIRED UP!
Creating jobs for the Poor and Middle Class
Is what Obama is all about

(8)BIRTHERS
FIRED UP!
OBAMA'S ON FIRE!
FIRED UP!
OBAMA'S ON FIRE!
FIRED UP!
HE'S FIRED UP!
FIRED UP!
HE'S FIRED UP!
FIRED UP!
Grade is Incomplete
FIRED UP!
Need 4 more years
FIRED UP!
To complete the job in creating more jobs
To calm all your tears and fears

(9)THE HATERS
FIRED UP!
OBAMA'S ON FIRE!
FIRED UP!
OBAMA'S ON FIRE!
FIRED UP!
HE'S FIRED UP!
FIRED UP!
HE'S FIRED UP!
FIRED UP!
God Is
FIRED UP!
In Control
The Right Wing think they know
it all but God is the ONE that Runs the Show

(10)REPUBLICON GOVENORS
FIRED UP!
OBAMA'S ON FIRE!
FIRED UP!
OBAMA'S ON FIRE!
FIRED UP!
HE'S FIRED UP!
FIRED UP!
HE'S FIRED UP!
FIRED UP!
Gov. Jan Brewer
Step back and give him space
And take your boney little finger
Out of my President's face

(11)ECONOMY
FIRED UP!
OBAMA'S ON FIRE!
FIRED UP!
OBAMA'S ON FIRE!
FIRED UP!
HE'S FIRED UP!
FIRED UP!
HE'S FIRED UP!
FIRED UP!
Hilda Solis
FIRED UP!
Labor Secretary
FIRED UP!
Public sector jobs, nurses,
Teachers, fire and the police

(12)ECONOMY
FIRED UP!
OBAMA'S ON FIRE!
FIRED UP!
OBAMA'S ON FIRE!
FIRED UP!
HE'S FIRED UP!
FIRED UP!
HE'S FIRED UP!
FIRED UP!
Manufacturing jobs
FIRED UP!
Made in the USA
FIRED UP!
Ford, Jazz, and apple pie
Is the old-fashioned American way

(13)EDUCATION
FIRED UP!
OBAMA'S ON FIRE!
FIRED UP!
OBAMA'S ON FIRE!
FIRED UP!
HE'S FIRED UP!
FIRED UP!
HE'S FIRED UP!
FIRED UP!
Race to the Top
FIRED UP!
That sets the high bar
FIRED UP!
A belated birthday present from
NASA and Curiosity landed on Mars

(14)EPA (Disaster Relief)
FIRED UP!
OBAMA'S ON FIRE!
FIRED UP!
OBAMA'S ON FIRE!
FIRED UP!
HE'S FIRED UP!
FIRED UP!
HE'S FIRED UP!
FIRED UP!
The President invest
FIRED UP!
In Renewable Energy
FIRED UP!
Federal Green Agencies to decrease
The effects of Global Warming

(15)FOREIGN POLICY
FIRED UP!
OBAMA'S ON FIRE!
FIRED UP!
OBAMA'S ON FIRE!
FIRED UP!
HE'S FIRED UP!
FIRED UP!
HE'S FIRED UP!
FIRED UP!
Awarded the
FIRED UP!
Nobel Peace Prize
FIRED UP!
Gave the Prize Money
To several of his favorite Charities

(16)MILITARY and VETERANS
FIRED UP!
OBAMA'S ON FIRE!
FIRED UP!
OBAMA'S ON FIRE!
FIRED UP!
HE'S FIRED UP!
FIRED UP!
HE'S FIRED UP!
FIRED UP!
Established a New
FIRED UP!
Task Force to assist
FIRED UP!
For Federal contracts and improve access
To all our Veterans who own a Business

(17)MITT ROMNEY
FIRED UP!
OBAMA'S ON FIRE!
FIRED UP!
OBAMA'S ON FIRE!
FIRED UP!
HE'S FIRED UP!
FIRED UP!
HE'S FIRED UP!
FIRED UP!
Obama Ordered
FIRED UP!
The closing of
FIRED UP!
Tax safe havens
For business tax evaders

(18)MITT ROMNEY
FIRED UP!
OBAMA'S ON FIRE!
FIRED UP!
OBAMA'S ON FIRE!
FIRED UP!
HE'S FIRED UP!
FIRED UP!
HE'S FIRED UP!
FIRED UP!
We ought to stop
FIRED UP!
Overseas call centers
FIRED UP!
To Create More Insource jobs
For the American people to have and enter

(19)PAUL RYAN
FIRED UP!
OBAMA'S ON FIRE!
FIRED UP!
OBAMA'S ON FIRE!
FIRED UP!
HE'S FIRED UP!
FIRED UP!
HE'S FIRED UP!
FIRED UP!
Don't be fooled
By Paul Ryan's charm
His beliefs and policies are so extreme
Written and made to do you harm

(20)REPUBLICON'S CONVENTION 2012 (Tampa, Fl)
FIRED UP!
OBAMA'S ON FIRE!
FIRED UP!
OBAMA'S ON FIRE!
FIRED UP!
HE'S FIRED UP!
FIRED UP!
HE'S FIRED UP!
FIRED UP!
Didn't it seem
Rubio and Christie
Instead of Romney running for the presidency

(21)DEMOCRAIC WOMEN
FIRED UP!
OBAMA'S ON FIRE!
FIRED UP!
OBAMA'S ON FIRE!
FIRED UP!
HE'S FIRED UP!
FIRED UP!
HE'S FIRED UP!
FIRED UP!
Obama knows
FIRED UP!
What a woman need
Don't be taken by Ryan looks
Cause he's no Kennedy

(22)MISCELLANEOUS
FIRED UP!
OBAMA'S ON FIRE!
FIRED UP!
OBAMA'S ON FIRE!
FIRED UP!
HE'S FIRED UP!
FIRED UP!
HE'S FIRED UP!
FIRED UP!
5 Judges
FIRED UP!
Supreme Court
FIRED UP!
Upheld the Decision the Tea Party
The ones that came up short

(23)DEMOCRATIC CONVENTION 2012
FIRED UP!
JOE BIDEN'S ON FIRE!
FIRED UP!
JOE BIDEN'S ON FIRE!
FIRED UP!
HE'S FIRED UP!
FIRED UP!
HE'S FIRED UP!
FIRED UP!
Bin Laden is dead
FIRED UP!
GM is alive
FIRED UP!
Going FORWARD not Back,
let's give a HIGH *FIVE*
With Obama's Administration
we will SURVIVE

(24)NORTH CAROLINA, DNC 2012
FIRED UP!
BILL CLINTON'S ON FIRE!
FIRED UP!
BILL CLINTON'S ON FIRE!
FIRED UP!
HE'S FIRED UP!
FIRED UP!
HE'S FIRED UP!
FIRED UP!
Obama Passed
FIRED UP!
The Arithmetic Test
FIRED UP!
Don't want Double Down on Triple Down
So Re-elect Obama for the 2nd Round

(25)VOTER SUPPRESSION
FIRED UP!
OBAMA'S ON FIRE!
FIRED UP!
OBAMA'S ON FIRE!
FIRED UP!
HE'S FIRED UP!
FIRED UP!
HE'S FIRED UP!
FIRED UP!
Calling First Time Voters
FIRED UP!
'08 Voters coming back
FIRED UP!
If you haven't voted in over 4 years
Get your Democratic ballots and get on track

(26)GET-OUT-THE-VOTE (GOTV)

FIRED UP!
OBAMA'S ON FIRE!
FIRED UP!
OBAMA'S ON FIRE!
FIRED UP!
HE'S FIRED UP!
FIRED UP!
HE'S FIRED UP!
FIRED UP!
Don't STOP!
FIRED UP!
Keep on PUSHING!
FIRED UP!
We must mobilize to give
Obama that CHEATN' CUSHION

(27)GET-OUT-THE-VOTE (GOTV)

FIRED UP!
OBAMA'S ON FIRE!
FIRED UP!
OBAMA'S ON FIRE!
FIRED UP!
HE'S FIRED UP!
FIRED UP!
HE'S FIRED UP!
FIRED UP!
We're Much Better Off
FIRED UP!
Than 4 Years Ago
And Romney better not STOP
The funds for Big Bird and Elmo

(28)GET-OUT-THE-VOTE (GOTV)

FIRED UP!

OBAMA'S ON FIRE!

FIRED UP!

OBAMA'S ON FIRE!

FIRED UP!

HE'S FIRED UP!

FIRED UP!

HE'S FIRED UP!

FIRED UP!

OBAMA'S ON FIRE!

FIRED UP!

OBAMA'S ON FIRE!

FIRED UP!

HE'S FIRED UP!

FIRED UP!

HE'S FIRED UP!

FIRED UP!

HE'S FIRED UP!

FIRED UP! And READY TO GO! FIRED UP!

www.ingramcontent.com/pod-product-compliance
Lightning Source LLC
Chambersburg PA
CBHW060431050426
42449CB00009B/2238